Name	Wishes and Comments

Name	Wishes and Comments

Name	Wishes and Comments

Name	Wishes and Comments

Name	Wishes and Comments
Name	Wishes and Comments
Name	Wishes and Comments
Name	Wishes and Comments

Name

Wishes and Comments

Name

Wishes and Comments

Name

Wishes and Comments

Name

Wishes and Comments

Name	Wishes and Comments

Name	Wishes and Comments

Name	Wishes and Comments

Name	Wishes and Comments

Name	Wishes and Comments

Name	Wishes and Comments

Name	Wishes and Comments

Name	Wishes and Comments

Name	Wishes and Comments

Name	Wishes and Comments

Name	Wishes and Comments

Name	Wishes and Comments

Name	Wishes and Comments

Name	Wishes and Comments

Name	Wishes and Comments

Name	Wishes and Comments

Name	Wishes and Comments
Name	Wishes and Comments
Name	Wishes and Comments
Name	Wishes and Comments

Name	Wishes and Comments

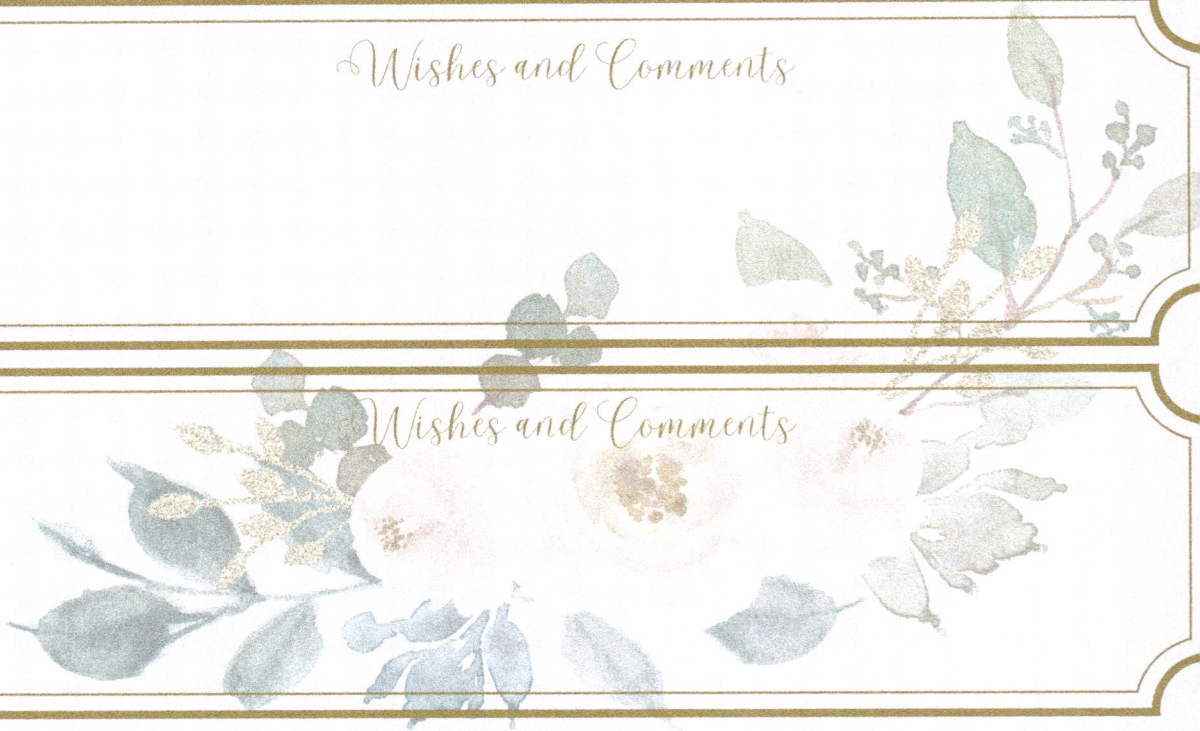

Name	Wishes and Comments

Name	Wishes and Comments

Name	Wishes and Comments

Name	Wishes and Comments

Name	Wishes and Comments

Name	Wishes and Comments

Name	Wishes and Comments

Name	Wishes and Comments

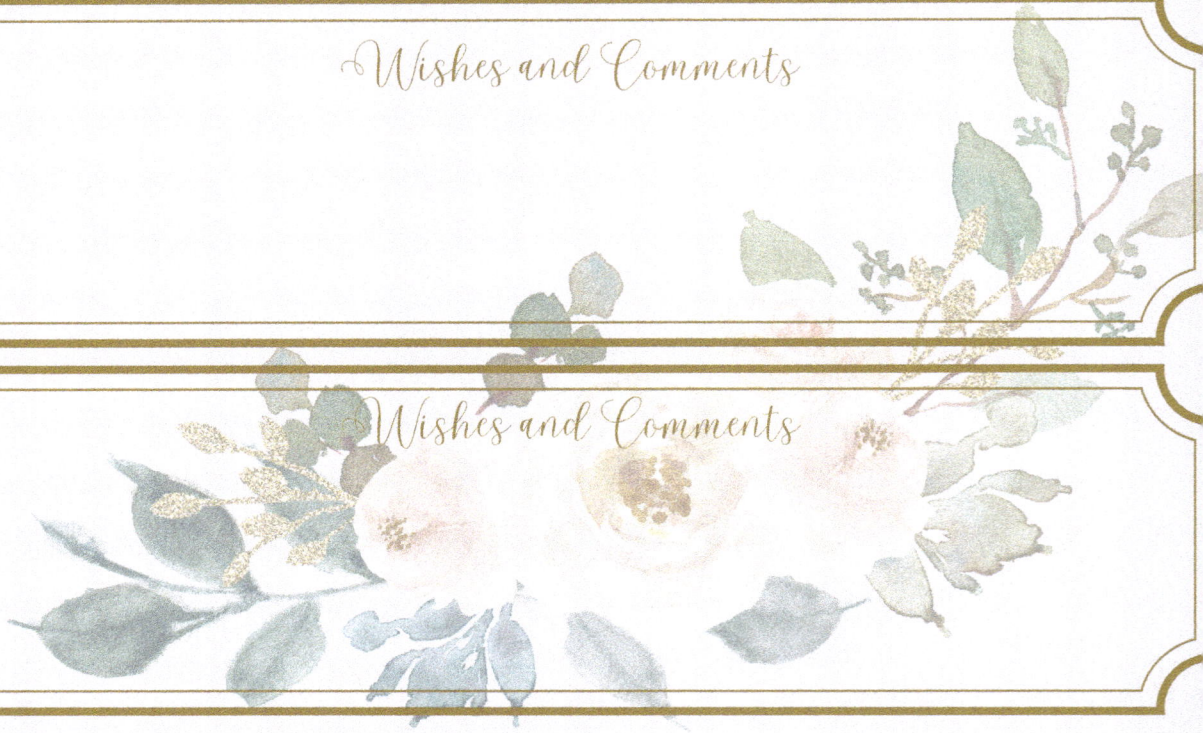

Name	Wishes and Comments

Name	Wishes and Comments

Name	Wishes and Comments

Name   Wishes and Comments

Name   Wishes and Comments

Name   Wishes and Comments

Name   Wishes and Comments

Name	Wishes and Comments

Name	Wishes and Comments

Name	Wishes and Comments

Name	Wishes and Comments

Name	Wishes and Comments

Name	Wishes and Comments

Name	Wishes and Comments

Name	Wishes and Comments

Name	Wishes and Comments

Name	Wishes and Comments

Name	Wishes and Comments

Name	Wishes and Comments

Name	Wishes and Comments

Name	Wishes and Comments

Name	Wishes and Comments

Name	Wishes and Comments

Name	Wishes and Comments

Name	Wishes and Comments

Name	Wishes and Comments

Name	Wishes and Comments

Name	Wishes and Comments

Name	Wishes and Comments

Name	Wishes and Comments

Name	Wishes and Comments

Name	Wishes and Comments

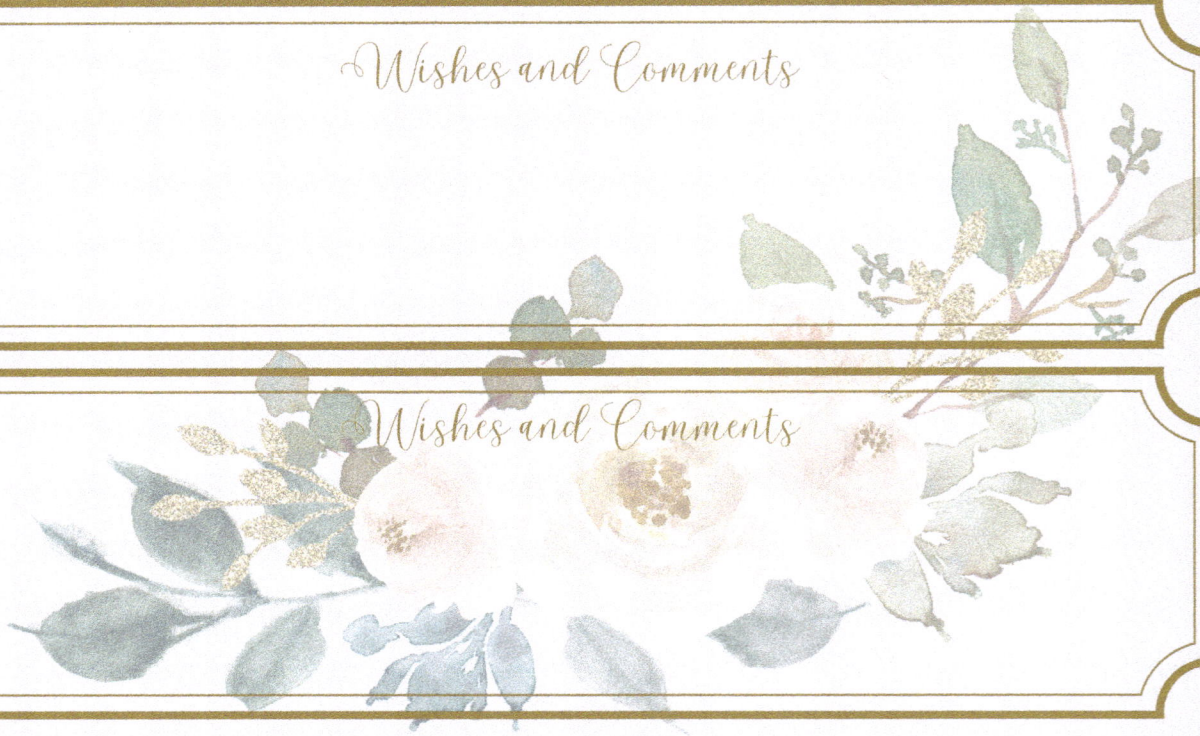

Name	Wishes and Comments

Name	Wishes and Comments

Name	Wishes and Comments

Name	Wishes and Comments

Name	Wishes and Comments

Name	Wishes and Comments

Name	Wishes and Comments

Name	Wishes and Comments

Name	Wishes and Comments

Name	Wishes and Comments

Name	Wishes and Comments

Name	Wishes and Comments

Name	Wishes and Comments

Name	Wishes and Comments

Name	Wishes and Comments

Name	Wishes and Comments

Name	Wishes and Comments

Name	Wishes and Comments

Name	Wishes and Comments

Name

Wishes and Comments

Name

Wishes and Comments

Name

Wishes and Comments

Name

Wishes and Comments

Name	Wishes and Comments
Name	Wishes and Comments
Name	Wishes and Comments
Name	Wishes and Comments

Name

Wishes and Comments

Name

Wishes and Comments

Name

Wishes and Comments

Name

Wishes and Comments

Name	Wishes and Comments

Name	Wishes and Comments

Name	Wishes and Comments

Name	Wishes and Comments

Name	Wishes and Comments

Name	Wishes and Comments

Name	Wishes and Comments

Name	Wishes and Comments

Name	Wishes and Comments

Name	Wishes and Comments

Name	Wishes and Comments

Name	Wishes and Comments

Name	Wishes and Comments

Name	Wishes and Comments

Name	Wishes and Comments

Name	Wishes and Comments

Name	Wishes and Comments

Name	Wishes and Comments

Name	Wishes and Comments

Name	Wishes and Comments

Name	Wishes and Comments

Name	Wishes and Comments

Name	Wishes and Comments

Name	Wishes and Comments

Name	Wishes and Comments

Name	Wishes and Comments

Name	Wishes and Comments

Name	Wishes and Comments

Name	Wishes and Comments

Name	Wishes and Comments

Name	Wishes and Comments

Name	Wishes and Comments

Name	Wishes and Comments
Name	Wishes and Comments
Name	Wishes and Comments
Name	Wishes and Comments

Name	Wishes and Comments
Name	Wishes and Comments
Name	Wishes and Comments
Name	Wishes and Comments

Name	Wishes and Comments

Name	Wishes and Comments

Name	Wishes and Comments

Name	Wishes and Comments

Name	Wishes and Comments

Name	Wishes and Comments

Name	Wishes and Comments

Name	Wishes and Comments

Name	Wishes and Comments

Name	Wishes and Comments

Name	Wishes and Comments

Name	Wishes and Comments

Name	Wishes and Comments

Name	Wishes and Comments

Name	Wishes and Comments

Name	Wishes and Comments

Name   Wishes and Comments

Name   Wishes and Comments

Name   Wishes and Comments

Name   Wishes and Comments

Name	Wishes and Comments

Name	Wishes and Comments

Name	Wishes and Comments

Name	Wishes and Comments

Name	Wishes and Comments

Name	Wishes and Comments

Name	Wishes and Comments

Name	Wishes and Comments

Name	Wishes and Comments

Name	Wishes and Comments

Name	Wishes and Comments

Name	Wishes and Comments

Name	Wishes and Comments

Name	Wishes and Comments

Name	Wishes and Comments

Name	Wishes and Comments

Name   Wishes and Comments

Name   Wishes and Comments

Name   Wishes and Comments

Name   Wishes and Comments

Name	Wishes and Comments

Name	Wishes and Comments

Name	Wishes and Comments

Name	Wishes and Comments

Name	Wishes and Comments

Name	Wishes and Comments

Name	Wishes and Comments

Name	Wishes and Comments

Name	Wishes and Comments

Name	Wishes and Comments

Name	Wishes and Comments

Name	Wishes and Comments

Name   Wishes and Comments

Name   Wishes and Comments

Name   Wishes and Comments

Name   Wishes and Comments

Name	Wishes and Comments

Name	Wishes and Comments

Name	Wishes and Comments

Name	Wishes and Comments

Name	Wishes and Comments

Name	Wishes and Comments

Name	Wishes and Comments

Name	Wishes and Comments

Name	Wishes and Comments

Name	Wishes and Comments

Name	Wishes and Comments

Name	Wishes and Comments

Name	Wishes and Comments

Name	Wishes and Comments

Name	Wishes and Comments

Name	Wishes and Comments

Name	Wishes and Comments

Name	Wishes and Comments

Name	Wishes and Comments

Name	Wishes and Comments

Name	Wishes and Comments

Name	Wishes and Comments

Name	Wishes and Comments

Name	Wishes and Comments

Name	Wishes and Comments

Name	Wishes and Comments

Name	Wishes and Comments

Name	Wishes and Comments

Name	Wishes and Comments

Name	Wishes and Comments

Name	Wishes and Comments

Name	Wishes and Comments

Name	Wishes and Comments

Name	Wishes and Comments

Name	Wishes and Comments

Name	Wishes and Comments

Name	Wishes and Comments

Name	Wishes and Comments

Name	Wishes and Comments

Name	Wishes and Comments

Name	Wishes and Comments
Name	Wishes and Comments
Name	Wishes and Comments
Name	Wishes and Comments

Name   Wishes and Comments

Name   Wishes and Comments

Name   Wishes and Comments

Name   Wishes and Comments

Name   Wishes and Comments

Name   Wishes and Comments

Name   Wishes and Comments

Name   Wishes and Comments

Name

Wishes and Comments

Name

Wishes and Comments

Name

Wishes and Comments

Name

Wishes and Comments

Name	Wishes and Comments

Name	Wishes and Comments

Name	Wishes and Comments

Name	Wishes and Comments

Name	Wishes and Comments

Name	Wishes and Comments

Name	Wishes and Comments

Name	Wishes and Comments

Name   Wishes and Comments

Name   Wishes and Comments

Name   Wishes and Comments

Name   Wishes and Comments

Name	Wishes and Comments

Name	Wishes and Comments

Name	Wishes and Comments

Name	Wishes and Comments

Name	Wishes and Comments

Name	Wishes and Comments

Name	Wishes and Comments

Name	Wishes and Comments

www.ingramcontent.com/pod-product-compliance
Lightning Source LLC
Chambersburg PA
CBHW041607260326
41914CB00012B/1414